THE BOOK OF UNREST

The Book of Unrest

POEMS BY

NICK MULGREW

UHLANGA

2022

First published in Durban, South Africa by uHlanga in 2022
UHLANGAPRESS.CO.ZA

Distributed outside Southern Africa by the African Books Collective
AFRICANBOOKSCOLLECTIVE.COM

ISBN: 978-0-620-98690-8

Edited by Francine Simon
Cover design and typesetting by Nick Mulgrew
Proofread by Karina Szczurek

The body text of this book is set in Garamond Premier Pro 11PT on 15PT

ACKNOWLEDGEMENTS

Earlier versions of some of these poems first appeared in the following publications: "A journalist in uMlazi" and "Siam, in some other place" in *The Johannesburg Review of Books*; "Ode to a boy hit by a kombi..." in *Stanzas*; "Ancestral recall" in the *Dundee University Review of the Arts*; and "Dogma" in *New Contrast*. "For two boys who died under Queen Nandi Drive" was shortlisted for the 2021 National Poetry Prize, and was published in the *Jack Journal*. Many friends have contributed to my own understanding of these poems. Thank you especially to Charles Buchan, Genna Gardini, Jennifer Jacobs, Athambile Masola, Tarn Painter-MacArthur, Francine Simon, Karina Szczurek, and Douglas Reid Skinner.

— N.M.

CONTENTS

i.m. S.A.J.
1960–2020

*"These are digressions, I know.
Hopeless detours. Evasions."*

– *LEWIS NKOSI,* Mating Birds

Dramatis personae

This person who is formed
from other people: where must I slouch
when the others go

off to sleep or to myth;
when the book is forgotten and couched
in rows of bending shelves

deep within or outwith?
Inside my self is a lonely place.
It is better to know

my self through a self, faced
with a pressure under which it must
liquify or shatter.

Most of a poem is words
in the way I am mostly water:
not the part that matters.

Ode to a time and place that is not this time and place

"He loved the climate and yearned for it away from Durban.
It made certain philosophies impossible to maintain, after all.
Sartre and de Beauvoir, Claude Lévi-Strauss, and others from the
Sorbonne wrote about the tropics, investigated their sad condition,
proclaimed on their behalf, classified and determined the varieties
of tropical consciousness. Yet they never could have prospered,
burned through so many cigarettes, and composed their endless
volumes at one hundred per cent humidity. The hot form of life,
the existence inside the body, precluded the other form."

— *IMRAAN COOVADIA,* Tales of the Metric System

I

A new message instants on the monitor you degauss for fun,
the pixels rummed and swaying like the palms
outside, where none of your attention lies.

You can't hear the song but you know its key
and modem hum like a lost father's voice; lilac-
clouded, you type to a girl until the morning rises

like damp. The air-conditioner wakes. Shrieking,
the neighbour begins her daily engagement
with the criminal vervets, their long, furred

fingers already slick with molten Swiss truffles. Snake-tongued,
the pitchfork's twines peek through the frame of the bedroom window.

დ

Disquiet, restlessness, or unrest, what does it matter.
The sky hangs milky with the char of fields
and factories. The sea froths brown, the estuary
glows blue: chemicals, candle-lit, plume overhill.

Difference lives between each defeated morning spent
scrubbing the veranda tiles: this was fields, years ago,
which used to be forest, which will be again.
The water carries dirt and soap and evaporates.

Bled out, the songololo hose now curls –
or is it the mamba as it unfurls
in green spitting fear? The kreepy-krawly heartbeat
drives you back inside, where there are no eyes but yours.

Standing by the pantry, skin radiant and radioactive,
you eat tinned guavas and cold Ultramel.
The empty bowl slips, yellow-wet, and shatters.
A raised hand can shush either a yawn or a yelp.

III

Who would leave Durban? the man who left Durban asks,
about all the men who left Durban to fulfil uncertain tasks.

The sun is a cartouche without graven name or image.
God, what is in this strange heat? The distant siren, a lineage

of moans; the breath of a world with spiders in its lungs.

Subsidence
– North Coast, April 2022

Receding now, the floodwater masquerades as ocean.
Every day the intertide rises further, approaching
the horizon in a parallel band: the coast is leaking grey;
even the dullest shades of blue desert the ruined bay.

We are surrounded by our surroundings, the foundations
now walls, the walls something else – rubble-cairns briskly masoned
and idle, memorials of brick immemorial.
Mangled fingers of rebar grasp from a rain-quarried hill

to the taunt of a fresh-sanded sky. A jumbo rakes by,
banking west, then north, to another where, another why.

A journalist in uMlazi

He was a journalist for ten years. During his training,
he was sent to uMlazi D Section. It was raining.
With colleague and broken Zulu he searched on the roadside
for anyone who knew of a girl who had been raped by
a man in the dark in a bush by the path by the stream.

He did not believe he would find that girl. He'd had a dream
his work might be meaningful, but there might be no meaning
in the diagonal world of green and mist and keening
people, who stared at him like the interloper he was:
hubristic boy, stunned sun-god, his wet ear caught in the conch.

The first person he spoke to, though, stood right next to the girl.
The second person he spoke to *was* the girl. But which girl?
the girl asked. There were five girls, in fact, with bulging eyes each,
wandering their neighbourhood in mauve matric hoodies.
They'd all been attacked on their way home from extra classes.

She took a maze of paths, showed him the dent in the grasses.
Yes, this is where it happened, she said, unable to blink
away tears from swelling, and welling, began to shrink
within herself. The journalist nodded, wrote in shorthand,
spoke in an impression of someone who could understand.

↩

The girl said she knew who he was. They all knew who *he* was.
Yes, he'd raped at least five girls her age. They knew who he was.
She had told laughing policewomen. They knew who he was.
The journalist asked, therefore, if he could write who he was.
No – due to legal reasons, he would not write who he was.

He was a journalist for ten years. This was his first day.
His mother picked him up from work. The next she did the same.

Choosing sides

I

In high school we wore uniforms, and since none of us wanted
to burn or darken, we picked our break-time teams by skin colour.
Charous against the rest – simple, save for the issue of Andy.
Ja nah, Kesh proclaimed, he's Indian enough. Come, let's dala.

For a happy half-decade we kept this secret arrangement,
the boarding boys filling in the blanks in our lighter ranks:
Ndweni, Ferreira, Vilakazi, Verdoorn and your boy
played Mannilal, both Pillays, the younger Vanniyar, and Yang.

We played at walking pace on the hockey fields, speaking in slurs,
friendships dressed in hatred's glimmering drag, as brothers do
to brothers when they cannot admit how they really feel.
How else were we supposed to bond? Newborn-frees without a clue

about how to live with each other, save for our assigned texts –
a vast history of misery, a litany of nos.
In twenty minutes between classes we opted to write our own
on the lines we crossed; proof that *we* would never come to blows.

"Ja bru, you remember it right," Kesh says as he goes to buy the next round.

"But you were quick to fright. When the other whites played, you were never around."

Sure, the first year we hung out, Kesh never called us friends – we were *connections*, playing thunee while the surfers in matric whipped groms with leather belts. On reflection, were my friends all just... protecting me? "Fuck, you ous never stop thinking about the past, hey." He checks his new watch. "Anyway, what y'alls drinking?"

It's good to see everyone again. This tray of beer is the closest thing we've had to a reunion in ten years – but it feels like someone's missing.

Wait, I ask – where's Andy? Kesh looks confused. "No bru, he went back to Taiwan. I scheme he hates us anyway – do you remember what his nickname was?"

I look into the oracle of fresh draught. I do, I say finally, remembering how we thought we were different to the other bullies, like that Israeli cricketer who punched Kesh for wearing a swastika to school on Diwali; he was the sort of white who always wanted an opportunity to be provoked, like that day Andy shiboboed him by the corner flag, and he knocked Andy flat with his red-ball fist, warning when he'd pulled himself back up: "I'll make your squint eyes round, Chingy."

Of course then we all rushed in, stick-insect Ferreira with his green-belt mae geri
and me...   Actually, I think I just stood there with my phone, filming
it so I could show it off later.   And God – isn't this poem the same thing?
Because – forgive me forgiving me – I'm not sure anymore where to go with this.
I don't know what benefit it brings. Perhaps some memories should stay repressed.

♠

In the life of night, kwaManilal, Kali mounts the lion.
With head and sword in burning hands, she looks toward Orion:

to her right a flame-bird rises; to her left, the pleasant place.
All that burns will come uncertain. All our pasts will be erased.

Home poem

The monkeys live in our gardens.
Our gardens are where the monkeys live.
The monkeys live around our house.
Our house is where the monkeys come.

When they speak it is like a door squeaking.
They hop from the banana palms.
The palms are in our garden.
The leaves bow at their knuckles.

The jasmine climbs the aloe tree:
the monkeys eat the white flowers.
The banana palm sprouts from the cliff
and clings as a soft, distant moss.

Our gardens are where the monkeys live.
The neighbour speaks open a window.
A glass bottle catches the sun.
When they scream it is like a door squeaking.

A littoral zone

As for the gift of a public bench
that leaves on sunwarmed skin
the imprint of its edge and gravelled pith,
remember: there is a furlong of this coast
that rests under no watchman's eyes.

At the river mouth where the river horse lay,
there are warrens of mangroves and sand,
depeopled like gardens are deweeded:
judiciously, and by hand.

Dear God, to wish for a life that is not this life,
and be found living a life that wishes that same wish –
this is heart-carrion. Shrugging, the lagoon tumbles
sunken teeth, rootless, toward the wastewater.

This froth and scum floats with life, but no,
these ancestors are not yours.
Unnamed, the bones stretch out from where they hide,
part-skeletons strung together by fishing line
and gwaai-breathed; they their own catch and release,

straining for the solace of a shoreline.
Where is your own relief?
There is the frame, but there is no seat.
Mistaken as driftwood, the beach regathers itself
and lies like an old towel, down for you, at your feet.

Morning poem

The pauper is damned by his ambition to sainthood.
In God's family, the siblings are tier-listed by their works.
What is in his portfolio but sin? It's all about him,
and that is only his problem.

Grounded by Gounden's, he eats what's left of last night
on the pavement of Umbilo Road. He does not hope
to cross the river ever again. In the north is only sin,
and every velvet morning

shouts it to him. He would stare at the ocean all night
in the hope that the sunrise will finally blind him
to the broken storm drains and the men
picking sneakers from the bin.

When the city wakes, the shelters shut their eyes.
Outside, we expose ourselves to the same cruel sky.

A brief history of shipwrecks

"They never returned to Mngazana, and the people
who now occupy the land know nothing about her,
her history or the whereabouts of her grave."

– *HAZEL CRAMPTON,* The Sunburnt Queen

I

The light rises from the surf.

An octopus basks on its own island
of salt-locked skull

until it is plucked
like a coconut from the cleft of the shore.

These things have washed up before.

↩

Ankles graze through the grazing grass
that designates field from beach.
But it is only rock under his horned feet,
no matter its past or pasture.
Sauntering from clay to coastal sand,
the breeze tickles the back of his hand.

Finally the baboon sun shines. From afar
he hopes for the glint of metal in the driftwood.
But he dares not approach the wreck-pieces
in fear that something has already called it home:
these dream-people and their children
have begun to enter his own.

The current is not the concern of the bay,
nor those distant and wooden nations
shattered like calf bone at the river mouths,
marrow seasoning the drips that drip
from wave-pounded pools and rocks.
He is convinced someone else's memories knock

from inside his own. He cannot shake it,
the image in his head of the child,
sun-bleached as rock, mousse-lipped
as the waves that delivered her.
Is it a vision, or is it history?
Empty-fisted, he turns his back on the sea.

Darkness before breath has no meaning other than its being.
It rises and bubbles and breaks as any unanswered question
at least for a moment, before light visits and sings.

One can make the mistake of thinking the sea only roils at its rim,
watching the sliding brine shatter and limn.
Still the thunder of water is an echo of last night's air.
She peers into the glass, and weeps as she combs her hair.

⊕

Centuries after the girl married away her line and name,
two boys from Durban North arrived shirtless in Coffee Bay.
Babalaased and delinquent, jeans bull-patterned with camping soot,
they rolled through the village with an empty tank and full boot.

Following the winding road of sea-cliff and shoeless shepherd,
they came to a clay-faced woman selling pineapples chequered
in ripening green. Identifying their kin, they chose those with golden skins,
believing them sweeter. The woman's eyes rolling

like summer clouds, she acquiesced. Feverishly the boys undressed
the rind and, leaning against the trunk, devoured the dank
and sun-warmed flesh, spitting rotten bits at their toes,
juice dripping from their proud three days of facial growth.

They asked the woman if she had anything else that was green.
Briefly looking down the road to make sure she hadn't been seen,
she procured from her haversack a Checkers bag full of weed.
The boys' eyes grew. "How much can we have?" they exclaimed. "We need,

like, everything you have. We're planning a long trip."
Wordlessly the woman smacked the Zam-Buk on her lips
and offered them the whole bag. When they reached out, she pulled back her hand.
"Ah," the driver said. "A problem. We just gave you our last ten rand."

Wordlessly the woman watched the boys instead open the hold
and stand back, gesturing it to her as if it were full of gold.
It wasn't, of course – only bubbled bodyboards, boxes and crates
of empties, a games console, and other assorted paperweights.

But the woman wasn't stupid – she'd grown her plants in her yard,
and everything had at least some value in a place this far
from what boys like this would call civilization, or something
equally as preposterous, given she was the one who had everything

they wanted: a home, the sun, a long and empty stretch of beach.
A place to be, in other words, not having to stretch to reach
every strand of pleasure they imagined they had rights to.
Eventually she shrugged and pointed: she'd take the PlayStation 2.

The driver smiled as he swiftly concluded the trade,
handing over the black cables and controllers in exchange
for the packet he promptly put to his nose and mouth.
Job done, the boys got back in the car for their trip further south

to Mgxotyeni, a name they couldn't say sober or slammed
into slurring by all of the heirloom pot in Pondoland.
Before they left, the driver leaned out the window to squint
at the woman's face, his own working out the puzzle in front of him.

"Hey, are you wearing contacts?" he asked. "Looks like your eyes are blue."
"Hayi bhuti," the woman closed them as she laughed: "Nam ndinobulungu."
At that the boys shrugged at each other, and took off, again lovesick
for their quarry. In the rear-view, the driver saw the woman shrink

until she was gone entirely, then sighed. "Well, that chick was rude."

"What?" said his passenger, sniffing the bag like glue.

"Did you hear what she called us?" "No, I don't speak Zulu."

"Bru, they don't speak Zulu here. Anyway, I think she called me umlungu."

"What does that mean?" the passenger asked, suddenly grave.

"Scum, man, sea scum, like the froth on top of the waves."

"Oh," the passenger said, and filed the fact deep in his mind, wondering how such a word could come from a face that looked so kind

and welcoming, and gave them everything they needed: taking the bud out the bag, he noticed it had already been deseeded.

Ode to a boy hit by a kombi near Edwin Swales Drive as we drove to the airport

And when I see you in my head it's as you float over the windscreen,
looking at something that is not there, as had Thomas past his finger
placed in Christ's wound, retracting from blood and skin, to linger
for a while as only chemical and spirit. Optics don't make marks?
The image is fleeting as life is: the cardholder's stance, your arc
forever upwards, forever dead, into an orbit unseen.
Highway-crosser in celestial tread, we were both fourteen.
In my half-life you have never ceased your ascent, some bary-
centre drifting further rogue, the weighted centre of me
cottoned, pulled loose as some toy you could never afford.

Later, an aeroplane lands south. People alight. People board.

Listicle: top five places in South Africa the People should expropriate

"Unless we can see our society in the light of other possible societies we cannot even understand how and why it works as it does, let alone judge it."

– RICHARD TURNER, *"The Necessity of Utopian Thinking"*

☙

There's an advert at the Kloof Street Seeff: Sol Kerzner's selling off some
real estate near Hout Bay; another small Lion's Head in and of the sun.
Obviously he's worried about black people taking it; regardless, it's insane
for someone to own a mountain nowadays, isn't it? So I say

let's go further. Forget boycott breakers, their lapping pretenders in the Lost City.
What has homeland gambling wrought but promise and bankruptcy?
A protest single, Bruce Springsteen sweating in the Velodrome,
prodding Queens for stalking the Pilanesberg's buck. To atone,

ten thousand whities shuffle on the Bridge of Time
while the Players walk on another course. But there is a better line
toward the resolution of this simulated history:
a thousand hotel rooms occupied by the poor, unlost and free.

4: EVERY AIRBNB IN CAPE TOWN

This old mosque has been renovated to a luxury spec,
including a rain-water shower in the steeple,
and solar panels... what do you mean, "minaret"?

Wealth is, as we have seen, power over other people.

∽

The further you go, the further it stays away:
peace and freedom are as far as the next town
from Ulundi – but here, between the purple of sunset
and in the haze of the morning that you leave,

it's easy to believe the crests of these hills
mark the borders of all existence.
Save your gaze from the new castle on the way out:
children and cattle still walk on the roads.

You risk nothing, and yet you don't risk it.
A circular tour circumscribes all that they haven't.
It's too difficult to dream when you're afraid
of your own face, ashen,

as the cowards amass on feed
and talkingly talk on radio,
toeing the line they suspended over
the ravine they call plateau.

Meanwhile you twiddle your thumbs on the glass,
and push the teeth around your plate:
"Oh, I suppose *something* should be said here,
but *I'm* not the one to say it."

I: THE ENTIRE COUNTRY

It's all very fun
until you get held to account,
because who doesn't dream themself accountable
until it actually starts to count?

Sertraline

It is an empty feeling in the sun,
not feeling its warmth.
Eyes closed against it,
the half-light exposes to blue.

A pigeon flies from the neighbour's wort-bush.
From its chest-noises
I hear it carry
a weight. Turning to view

          it, I don't.
          It is already too late.

Siam, in some other place

– Virginia Circle, 2018

Still the cane waves on the hills like an ocean in swell,
and the smoke is the dark spotlight.

In some other place it is not a pyre.
   I am sorry it is not here.

In the same place the children still stand by the circle.
In some other place this wouldn't have to be written.

Ancestral recall

I

Here is Shepstone Road, and here is the vinegar that runs from your mouth.

Here is your family car and your father idling in the front seat.

Here is his elbow broken, the gravel still under his skin.

Here again is the apple you ate this morning when you thought you'd be OK.

Here it is again! It looks like lemon pith, swimming in milk on the tarmac, yes:

here is the inside of you pooling and gliding into the gutter.

Here is the sky, and here is cumulus, and you are small in this empty carapace of this

here city on the bay, encrusted like fungus on a toe, cancer on a tongue and retching.

Here is the vagrant attracted, asking you for change while you divine water again.

Here is your wife, rubbing your back and telling him to please go away please.

Here he comes closer again and laughs as you yawn water again.

Here again is the shame, and here again is the shame.

God, God, God, it always comes back to this. You picture yourself dispensing wisdom
to a younger version of yourself; is it you at fourteen, or your unborn son?
If you have to sit in a strange shower an hour before a meeting, praying –
I am OK, I am OK, I am – the chances are you're not what you're saying,

When I was young a great-auntie told me the history of how her cousin died
drinking bottles of vinegar one night. The cupboards were bare. They'd run out of wine.
I remember this wrong, probably, so I pause in telling it, in sharing shame
that's not mine, although that shame is mine: the picture's the same, but not the frame.

It's bad faith to treat family stories as apocrypha, to bend them to your whim.
History isn't just what is remembered – things happened regardless of your knowing,
and they scar themselves on you as death did your heart, as the acid does your gullet,
as nail does oak when they write the myth on basement beams in dark Wood Street, then rot

in the same cemetery. You trace the lines between graves like the boughs of a birch.
There's your grandfather, and there's his. The stones, like teeth, push from the gums of the earth.

For two boys who died under Queen Nandi Drive

"All mercy deserted them."

– *RONNIE GOVENDER,* 1949

It was for the sake of TVs, the security guard said,
that thousands emerged from the corrugated hills.
It was late when the largest warehouse exploded.
The size of the smoke-plume could only be known
by the orange flame that rose beneath it,
a new bloom in the valley's cut palms,
that grew as large as the eyes that bore its witness.

The detritus left after our small apocalypse
was as meaningful as an eight-day week:
powder and soil; cardboard spontaneously confettied;
overturned containers, their slack jaws picked clean.
In the floral kingdom of plastic bags
the hi-vis vests recover first,
germinating on the bridge that still stood
despite the protestations of those who stood on it.

Forget the two boys who lie under that loose
and concrete blanket. Remember: it was for TVs
that *they* came – so someone had said – and because
it was such a simple thing for which they had come,
it was one also to overlook them
among the carrion of cold-chain centres
and the ribcages of factories –
things that someone still cared for.

But only things are still, and still the things are,
parentless mannequins discarded
outside the city's ransacked shopfront.
How naïve it is to expect care in death
when there is no care in life.
Sanctified, the sweeping brooms sweep out
the remains of things, urned, or interred in mind –
ash is only dust with provenance.

Prayer

Sea-cloud, patient tide, you wait for me,
and under your blanket it is warm.
The dark focuses the eye to where it is not:
ships seam through the velvet pulled taut;
air-drunk, the moon stays on its side of the bed.

How do we all fit here, in fitful sleep?
Even the earth contracts as it cools.
The car-lamps, open-shuttered, stream
eternally across the coast's vision; ghostly,
seafoam cavalry pound the waves into mist.

Dogma

Religion is a metaphor for existence,
just as I am for myself;
a clear sky over the ocean for breath.

But the air is never clear in Durban, is it?
I swim out to the shark nets
and turn in the warm water to look back,

and over the city and over my birth is
a grey-brown pall, transparent
and agitated as it is below.

What fish are caught in the nets tickling at my toes?
I cannot know from what I'm
protected or what is killed in my name,

and yet I have spent my life in this water
dreaming of the welcome pull
of its warm and grey-brown transparency;

all those Sundays, rash vests and two-litre Coke
bottles filled to brims with foam,
wide-throated and regurgitated whole

back into the foamed waves from which they were pulled.
In the rock pools a child nets for minnows.
She takes them home in a plastic cup and

watches them swim until they die.

I saw the face of Christ in the soft silt
left by the flood in my parents' kitchen
the week after a man wrapped a brick from
our crumbling boundary wall in a beach towel
we had left on the washing line and smashed
a window pane and, upon hearing the
alarm which we had only last week
learned how to activate, slashed himself
on the glass, leaving a trail of his blood
into the living depths of the garden.

The floods were fast and sullen.
This isn't a metaphor –
this is just the way floods are.

My parents and I took up brooms: scrapping
they swept the brown-grey rain out the garage;
I, round the back, purged rain into the pool,
which then overflowed and pushed itself back.
The next morning I spent the sunlight picking
up weavers' nests and palm fronds from the lawn.
At the pool's bottom lay two small white eggs.
One was whole; the other holed, its insides
chalk-bleached and clean as my nine-year-old soul.
I buried them both in the soft brown loam

under the lemon tree with
the bodies of my parrots.
The lemon tree bore no fruit.

The water had made the earth soft at last,
so after the man bled in the garden
our neighbours installed metal spikes in
the mulch on their side of the boundary wall,
hidden from sight by the trees they called theirs.
Of course I only discovered this fact
when I hit an old tennis ball for six
into their circumscribed square of brown loam
and, jumping the wall, missed every point by
about the length of the line of a poem.

This, I must repeat, isn't
metaphor. This is not some
thing to ascribe a meaning to.

This is just what happens.

It is refusal we all practise, waterproof skin,
  dark thoughts in our pith.
All of our selves are intentional, constructed
  from memory, myth

and ash, crossed onto the hot forehead of a
  child who does not yet know what
sin is, not to speak of memory or myth, only
  the shark caught and gut

on a steel table in the baking sun while
  the sugar cane burns around
him. He does not yet know that his home
  and garden are built on the soft ground

named for the son of a man who brought over
  the ancestors of his neighbours
from their own home and sullen coast to
  plant and tend these acres.

Where would heaven be if heaven had a view
  of hell?
This is what happens when we make meaning
  of our selves.

◦∋

I too left that coast at seventeen, but I am not Fernando.
But then neither was he, nor Ricardo, Álvaro, Alberto.
Oh, to be the elderly child stuck in the city of their mother,
dreaming only the dreams they dream; only the dreams of others.

Draft

Later, he wrote, rewriting is unwriting,
and a moment later rewrote it:
writing is unwriting.

NOTES

p.24, "A littoral zone" – the epigraph from Sally-Ann Murray is from her collection *Open Season* (2006).

p.35, "Listicle..." – the epigraph from Richard Turner is from an essay in *The Eye of the Needle* (1972). The italicised line in "Every Airbnb in Cape Town" is taken from "The Politics of Socialism", another essay in the same book.

p.42, "Siam..." – Siam is a woman's name.

p.45, "For two boys..." – the epigraph from Ronnie Govender is from his play *1949* (1994), later collected in *Interplay* (2007).

p.48, "Dogma" – the epigraph from Douglas Livingstone is from his collection *Eyes Closed Against the Sun* (1970); the epigraph from Alberto Caeiro is from Jonathan Griffin's translations of the *Selected Poems* of Fernando Pessoa (1974) – Caeiro is one of Pessoa's innumerable heteronyms, including (depending on who you ask) Pessoa himself.

POETRY FOR THE PEOPLE

— RECENT RELEASES —

A Short Treatise on Mortality by Douglas Reid Skinner

Peach Country by Nondwe Mpuma

Unam Wena ngu Mthunzikazi A. Mbungwana

Jesus Thesis and Other Critical Fabulations by Kopano Maroga
SHORTLISTED FOR THE 2022 NIHSS AWARD FOR BEST POETRY

— RECENTLY-AWARD-WINNING TITLES —

An Illuminated Darkness by Jacques Coetzee
WINNER OF THE 2022 INGRID JONKER PRIZE

Ilifa ngu Athambile Masola
WINNER OF THE 2022 NIHSS AWARD FOR BEST POETRY

All the Places by Musawenkosi Khanyile
WINNER OF THE 2021 NIHSS AWARD FOR BEST POETRY
WINNER OF THE 2020 SOUTH AFRICAN LITERARY AWARD FOR POETRY

Everything is a Deathly Flower by Maneo Mohale
WINNER OF THE 2020 GLENNA LUSCHEI PRIZE FOR AFRICAN POETRY
FINALIST FOR THE 2020 INGRID JONKER PRIZE

Zikr by Saaleha Idrees Bamjee
WINNER OF THE 2020 INGRID JONKER PRIZE

AVAILABLE FROM GOOD BOOKSTORES IN SOUTH AFRICA & NAMIBIA
& FROM THE AFRICAN BOOKS COLLECTIVE ELSEWHERE

UHLANGAPRESS.CO.ZA

Printed in the United States
by Baker & Taylor Publisher Services